--THE WORLD'S BEST BOOK OF RIDDLES

BUSTER BOOKS

Illustrated by
Andrew Pinder

Compiled by Bryony Davies
Edited by Lara Murphy and Hannah Daffern
Designed by Jade Moore
Cover design by Angie Allison

First published in Great Britain in 2024 by Buster Books,
an imprint of Michael O'Mara Books Limited,
9 Lion Yard, Tremadoc Road, London SW4 7NQ

W www.mombooks.com/buster

f Buster Books

𝕏 @BusterBooks

O @buster_books

A CIP catalogue record for this book is available from the British Library.

ISBN: 978-1-78055-999-5

1 3 5 7 9 10 8 6 4 2

This product is made of material from well-managed, FSC®-certified
forests and other controlled sources. The manufacturing processes
conform to the environmental regulations of the country of origin.

Printed and bound in May 2024 by
CPI Group (UK) Ltd, Croydon, CR0 4YY.

MIX
Paper | Supporting
responsible forestry
FSC® C171272

Introduction

Welcome to the world's BEST BOOK of riddles, a rollercoaster ride of puzzle challenges designed to boggle your brain!

Test your problem-solving powers with clever conundrums, ridiculous riddles and baffling brainteasers. Once you've cracked them, why not set your friends and family the challenge, too?

Giving your brain a workout is as important as exercise for your body. The more puzzles you solve, the bigger the brain will grow, so what are you waiting for? Dive in and get those brain cogs into gear!

All the answers are in the back of the book so if you need some extra help, take a peek and discover more about how riddles are solved. The more you learn to think like a Master Riddler, the quicker you'll get at cracking riddles.

Happy riddle-solving!

1. I'm as strong as ten people and as long as ten people, yet one person can carry me. What am I?

2. What has many rings but no fingers?

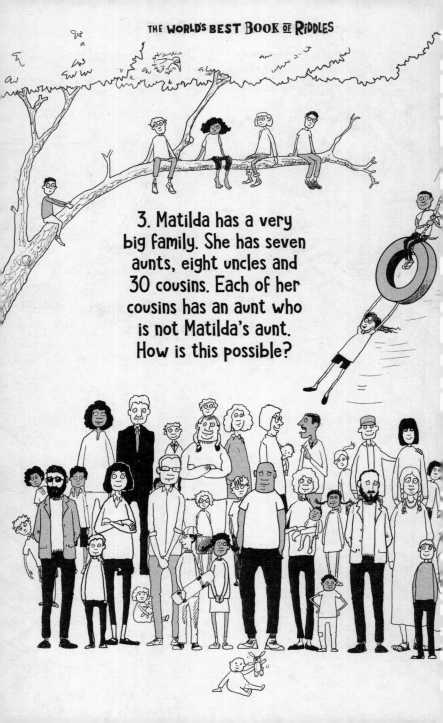

3. Matilda has a very big family. She has seven aunts, eight uncles and 30 cousins. Each of her cousins has an aunt who is not Matilda's aunt. How is this possible?

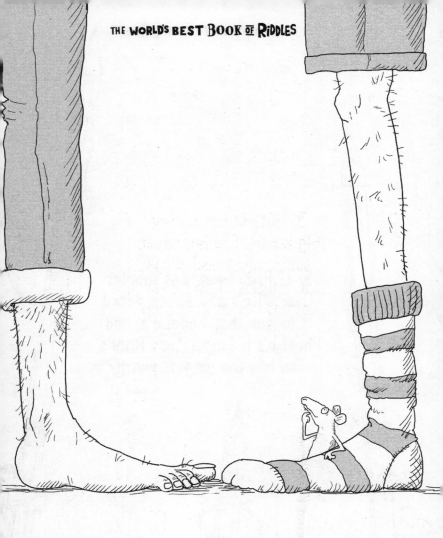

4. What is two feet long but can be all different sizes?

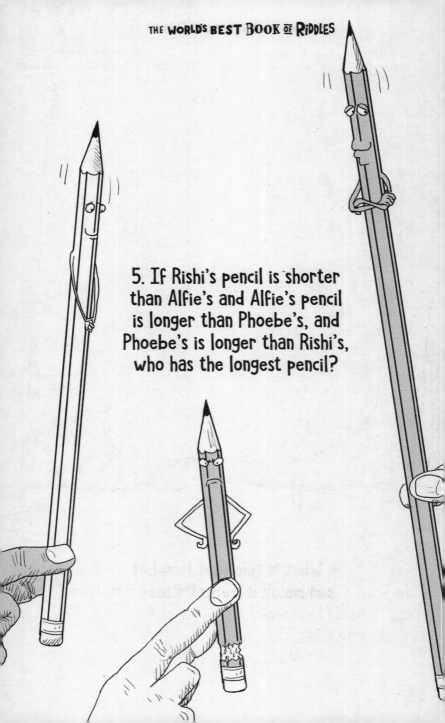

5. If Rishi's pencil is shorter than Alfie's and Alfie's pencil is longer than Phoebe's, and Phoebe's is longer than Rishi's, who has the longest pencil?

6. Sophia is climbing a ladder that is 7 metres (23 feet) high when she loses her footing, slips and falls. She walks away uninjured. How can this be?

7. A mother has two sons who share the same birthday and are born in the same year, but they are not twins. How is this possible?

8. Which word becomes shorter when you add two letters to it?

9. A magician gestures to a bookshelf filled with books and says to a child in the audience: "If you can find the banknote that's hidden between pages 79 and 80 of one of the books on these shelves within 30 seconds, you can keep the money."

The child shakes their head and says, "That's impossible."

Why?

11. What has a face but no eyes?

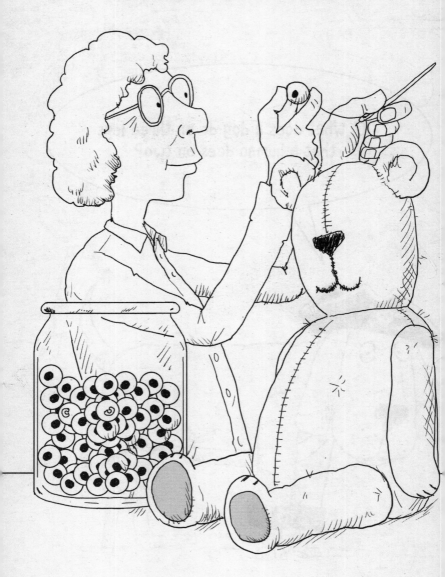

12. What's harder to catch
the faster you run?

14. I cross a small bridge and I help those that cannot see very well. What am I?

15. Two's company, three's a crowd. What do four and five make?

16. What kind of coat can only be put on when wet, and is no use for keeping out the cold?

17. A polar bear walks 5 kilometres
(3.1 miles) north and then 4 kilometres
(2.5 miles) south, but ends up 9 kilometres
(5.6 miles) from where it started.
How is that possible?

19. Shelina takes her dog for a walk. It doesn't walk behind her, in front of her or to one side of her. It isn't above her or below her, and she isn't carrying it. So where is it?

20. I have a head and a tail, but no body. I'm not a snake. What am I?

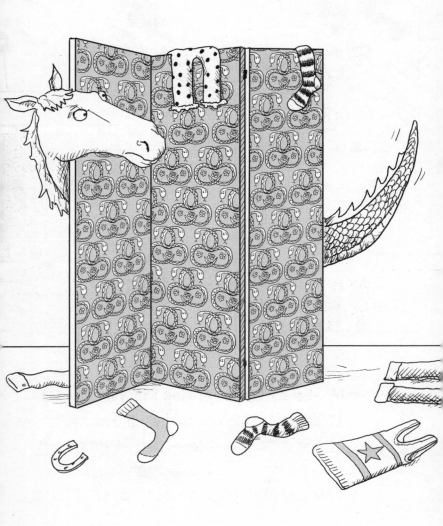

21. If the alphabet goes from A to Z, what goes from Z to A?

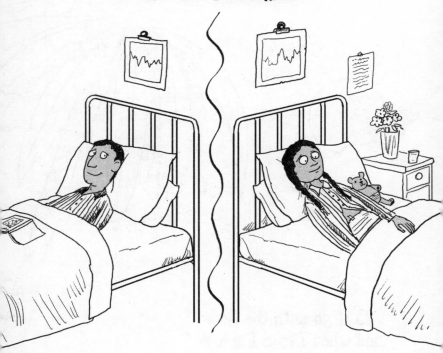

22. Jamila's brother went to the hospital to have his tonsils out. A week later, her sister went to hospital to have her appendix removed. A month later, Jamila needed to have something removed from her head, but she didn't go to hospital. Why?

23. I go with the flow,
and when I'm in I'm high,
but when I'm out I'm low.
What am I?

25. If you feed me I will live, but if you water me I will die. What am I?

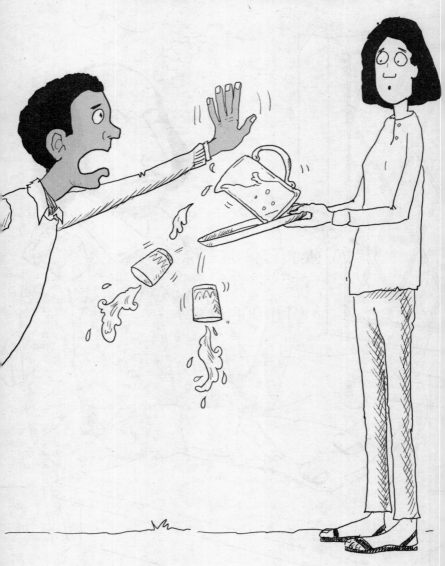

26. What food do the following letters spell out?

POTOOOOOOOO

28. What creature can travel as far as it likes but never leaves home?

30. Six boys stood under a small umbrella but none of them got their hair wet. How?

31. What seven-letter word leaves seven even when you take two letters away?

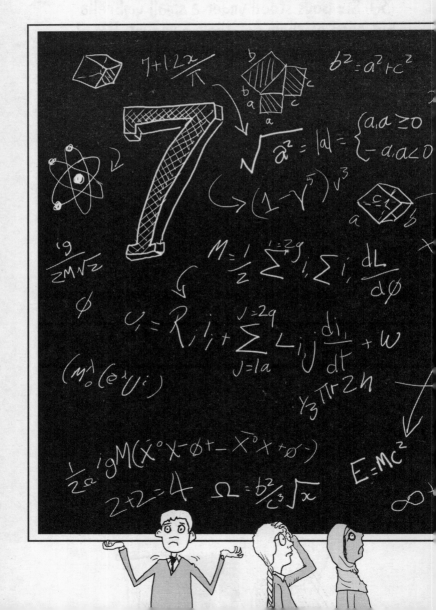

32. What can you put between five and six to make a number greater than five but less than six?

33. What grows even though it isn't alive?

34. Double it then multiply it by four. Then divide it by eight and you'll have it once more. What number is it?

It looks like some sort of magical curse ...

35. What gets wetter the more it dries?

36. How many books can you put into an empty box?

37. What animal can jump higher than a building?

38. I have keys, but they don't open locks. You can enter, but you can't exit – although, you can escape! What am I?

39. A blackberry bush has an average of six branches, with 12 twigs on each branch and 24 fruits on each twig. How many blueberries would grow on one bush?

40. What cup can't you drink from?

41. What is there when you are quiet, but breaks as soon as you speak?

42. What has eyes but cannot see,
a tongue but can't speak,
and is no use on its own?

43. Kerepakupai Merú in Venezuela, also known as Angel Falls, is the world's tallest waterfall. What was the tallest waterfall in the world before it was discovered?

44. I'm very tall with one blinking eye, and I beam at passers-by. But I'm not being friendly, there's danger nearby. What am I?

45. What phrase is shown below?

SECRET

SECRET

SECRET

46. Nellie was at her cousin's ninth birthday party when someone asked her how old she was. She replied, "In two years' time I will be twice as old as I was five years ago." How old is she?

47. There's only one place where Friday comes before Thursday? Where is it?

48. A brother and sister take their dog for a walk. The sister jogs at an average of 7 km/h (4.3 mi/h), while the brother walks at 5 km/h (3 mi/h). The dog runs back and forth between them at a constant pace of 9 km/h (5.6 mi/h) without stopping.

After an hour, how far will the dog have run?

49. Nikhil and Benji are best friends who love playing sport. Nikhil plays tennis on days that have an S in their name. Benji plays hockey on days that have an M in their name.

What is the only day of the week that neither of them plays sport?

50. Your Aunt Alisha's brother is related to you, but he's not your uncle. Who could he be?

51. What has a bed but never sleeps, and a mouth but never speaks?

52. There are two trucks carrying furniture between London and Edinburgh. One truck leaves London on Tuesday morning at 9 am, and travels at 63 km/h (39 mi/h). The other truck leaves London on Tuesday at 11.30 am, and travels at 70 km/h (44 mi/h). Which truck will be nearer to Edinburgh when they pass each other?

53. Can you work out what phrase is written in code below?

CCCCCCC

54. It takes three and a half minutes to fry an egg. How long does it take to fry four eggs?

55. You can make it, but you can't see it or hold it. What is it?

56. Which of the following sentences is correct?
"Lola sat on the bigger half of the sofa" or
"Lola sat on the biggest half of the sofa"?

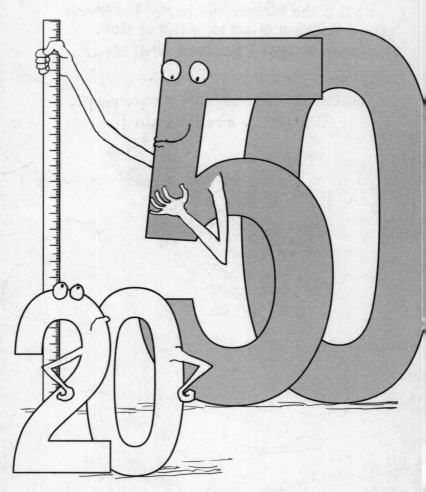

59. I am bigger than 20 but smaller than 50, and when I'm spelt out my letters are in alphabetical order. What number am I?

60. Some toadstools are growing in a clearing. What is the minimum number of toadstools there can be if a red toadstool is growing to the left of a white toadstool; a white toadstool is growing to the left of a white toadstool; and two white toadstools are growing to the right of a red toadstool?

61. What can run but cannot walk?

62. Sophia was sitting in class at school when her teacher asked her: "How many seconds are there in a year?"

Sophia answered, "Twelve."

The teacher paused then said that she was right. How can that be?

$60 \times 60 = x$

$x \times 24 = y$

$y \times 365 = z$

63. Farmer Jane had a stall at the market where she sold apples. One cold winter morning she only had three customers. The first one said: "I'll buy half your apples and half an apple more."

Her second customer said the same thing.

Her third customer only asked for one apple.

Farmer Jane managed to give each customer what they wanted without cutting a single apple in half. How many apples did she have on her stall?

64. Can you work out what word is shown below?

BOLT

TH

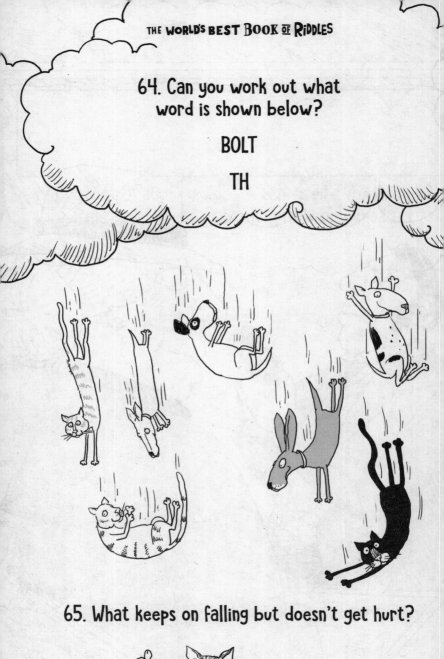

65. What keeps on falling but doesn't get hurt?

66. I can point the way when I'm full, but when I'm empty I lie still. I'm useless when it's hot but I'll keep you warm when it's chilly. What am I?

67. You are standing in front of a sink full of water.
You have a bowl, a bottle, a teaspoon and a jug.
What is the quickest way to empty the sink?

68. I can be told or played, cracked or made. What am I?

69. When Florence was eight, her sister was half her age. Now Florence is 14. How old is her sister?

70. Without my first two letters
I'm a large primate. Without my first
three letters I'm a subject in school.
If you take away my first four letters
I'm the letter 'e'. What word am I?

71. Henry is bored in a lesson. There are 25 mice around him, constantly on the move, but no one is paying them any attention. How could this be?

72. What runs up and down the stairs without moving?

73. You are trapped in the hall of a haunted castle. There is no way out except by going through one of the three doors that are in front of you. Behind the first door is a child-eating ogre. Behind the second is a hungry werewolf. Behind the third door is a tiger that hasn't had any food for four years.

Which door do you choose to go through to escape the castle without being eaten?

74. What is always coming but never arrives?

75. If a red house is made of red bricks,
and a brown house is made of brown bricks,
what is a greenhouse made of?

76. A hungry snail is trying to climb a wall to reach the vegetable patch behind. The wall is 12 bricks high. Each time the snail manages to climb up three bricks, it then loses its grip and slides back down two bricks. Every time that it climbs up and then slides back, it takes an hour. How long does it take the snail to reach the top of the wall?

77. Can you spell out an odd number that becomes even if you remove one letter?

78. Dan's mother has three sons. The oldest is called James and the middle one is called Jasper. What is the youngest called?

79. To screw a screw into a small piece of wood with your right hand, you turn the screwdriver clockwise. To remove the screw you hold it still and turn the piece of wood with your left hand instead. Which way do you turn the wood?

80. What flies but doesn't have wings?

81. You have planted a big patch of sunflower seeds in your back garden. Every day, the number of flowers doubles. If it takes 52 days for the flowers to fill the flower patch, how many days would it take for them to fill half the flower patch?

82. What starts off on four 'legs', uses two legs as it gets older, and ends up using three 'legs'?

83. I'm a seven-letter word, but if you take away four of my letters, only one is left. You could say I'm the queen of the jungle. What am I?

84. What has a back and four legs but can't walk?

85. You take your pet rabbit to the vet, and the vet gives you four pills. She tells you that you need to give your rabbit one pill every half hour. How long do the pills last?

R.I.P.

86. Tread on us while we're alive and we are quiet, but tread on us when we are dead and we make a noise! What are we?

87. What can you add to a bucket
of water to make it lighter?

88. Can you name three days that come straight after each other without saying either Monday, Wednesday or Friday?

91. I'm light as a feather and you can scrunch me in your hand, but be careful, I can cut you! What am I?

92. I'm at the centre of gravity, and you can find me in Venus, but not Mars. What am I?

93. Farah has been hired to paint the numbers 1 to 100 on 100 hotel room doors. How many times will she paint the number 8?

94. You can make me, save me, raise me and change me. What am I?

95. Which word is the odd one out in the following sentence?

'You are fun.'

96. What can you catch but not throw?

97. I'm hard like a stone and I grow on your body. What am I?

98. I can turn one person into two. What am I?

99. There's a fruit bowl on Grandma's table containing two types of fruit. If you jumble up the letters of one fruit, you can spell the other. What are the two fruits?

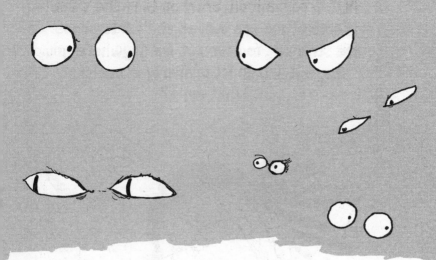

100. The more there is of me the less you see.
What am I?

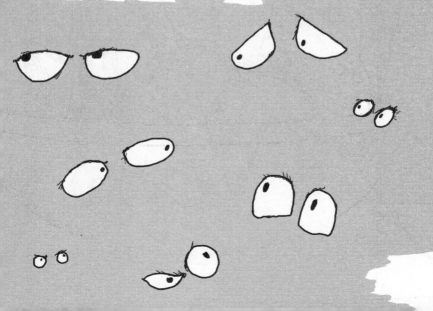

101. I come in different shapes and sizes. Parts of me are curved and parts of me are straight. You can put me anywhere you like, but I only fit properly in one spot. What am I?

102. I can be a bird or a fruit. What am I?

103. On Monday, Geoffrey the gigantic guinea pig eats one carrot. On Tuesday he eats two carrots, and on Wednesday he eats four. If he continues to follow this pattern, how many carrots does he eat in a week?

104. What kind of work is impossible to do at school?

105. I guide people all around the world, but all I can do is point. What am I?

106. What kind of flower doesn't have petals?

107. What kind of car is spelled the same backwards and forwards?

108. What has 13 hearts but no other organs?

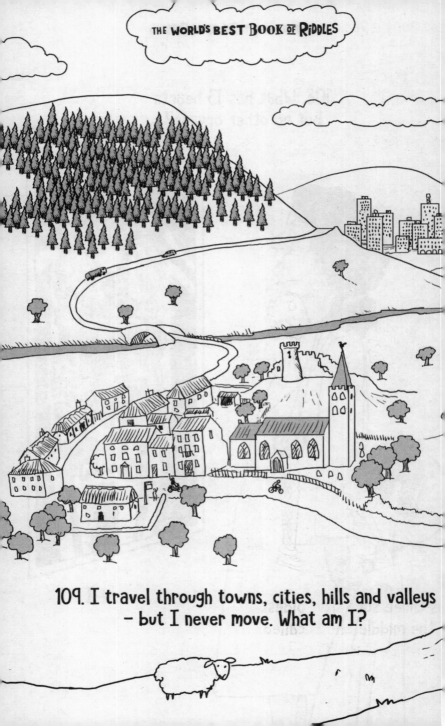

109. I travel through towns, cities, hills and valleys
– but I never move. What am I?

110. At the Sunrise Café, everything on the menu has to follow one rule. They serve pizza but not burgers, carrot cake but not chocolate cake, and noodles but not salad. What is the rule?

111. I'm found on land and at sea, although you can't see me. You can't hold me either, but you can use me and hear me. What am I?

112. At the funfair, Isla, Billy, Daniel, Emma and Freddie had to guess the number of sweets in a small jar. Isla guessed 20, Billy guessed 21, Daniel guessed 22, Emma guessed 17 and Freddie guessed 16. One person was wrong by four, another person was wrong by three, one by one, another by two and one person was correct. How many sweets were there?

113. What's easy to get into but hard to get out of?

114. This is a word in the English language: the first two letters refer to a male, the first three letters refer to a female, the first four letters describes someone great, while the entire word describes a brilliant woman. What is the word?

115. What begins with T, ends with T, and has T inside it?

116. I can fly through the air, travelling halfway across the world each year in search of warmth. But I am also something you do to your food. What am I?

117. What goes up but never down?

118. You are in a room with three monkeys. One has a stick, one has a banana and one has nothing. Who is the smartest primate?

119. What uses borrowed feathers to fly through the air?

120. What sort of driver only goes round in circles?

121. When is it correct to say, "I is"?

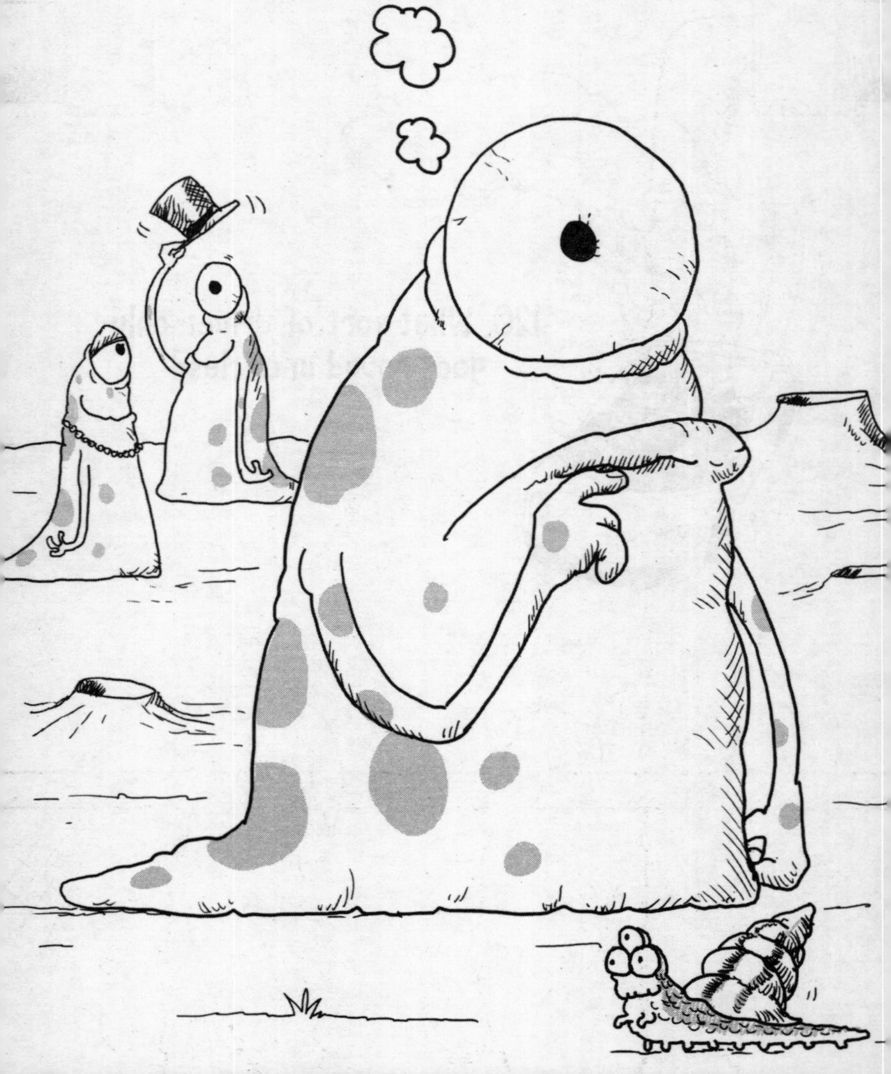

122. What is round and deep like a bowl, but impossible to fill up with water?

123. Which animal is one third cow and half goat?

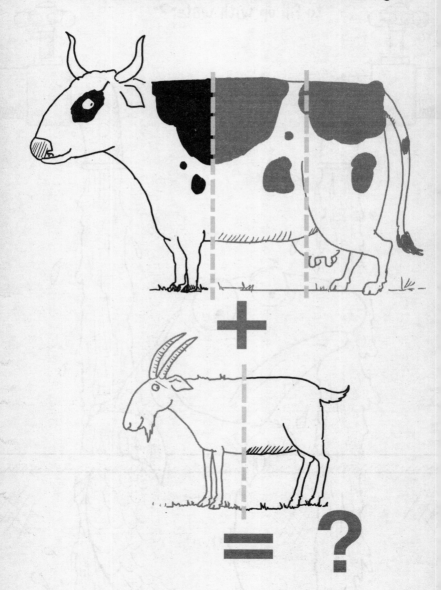

124. At night they arrive without an invitation, and they go in the morning without being taken. What are they?

125. Mo was 12 the day before yesterday, and next year he'll turn 15. How is this possible?

126. I am the beginning of the end and the end of time and space. I am essential to creation, and I am at either side of every place. What am I?

127. You can peel my skin off and I won't cry – but you might! What am I?

128. Jack arrived at the riverbank with his pet dragon, a chicken and a bag of grain. He found a small boat which he could row across to the other side, but it was only big enough to carry him and one other thing at the same time.

The dragon and the chicken couldn't be left alone together, or one would eat the other, and neither could the chicken and the grain, or there would be no grain left.

How did Jack get everything safely across the river?

129. What flies around when it is created, lies around during its lifetime and runs away when it dies?

130. Farmer Albert and Farmer Kate take their dog, Hector, out to their barn to check on their lambs. They have two ewes and three baby lambs safe and warm in the barn. They also find their cat, Star, fast asleep in the hay. How many feet are there in the barn?

131. What six-letter word is a vegetable, and if you chop the word in half you are left with the name of an item that you can cook it in?

132. What kind of ship can unite enemies?

133. Nobody can empty me, but I never stay full for long. What am I?

134. I wear a cap but I don't have a head, mistake me for another and you might end up dead! What am I?

135. I'm handy around the home, but not often on display. I've been known to be sat on, but I'm not a chair. I've got a handle, but I'm not a door. I've got bristles, but I'm not a toothbrush. What am I?

136. Four friends are taking part in a cycle race. Sally finishes four minutes ahead of Sophie. Phil finishes eight minutes ahead of Matthew. Matthew took six more minutes than Sally to finish the race. What order do they cross the finish line in?

137. A ship's anchor dangles from a hole in its bow. At low tide, the anchor is 1 metre (3.2 feet) below the surface of the water. At high tide, when the water rises by 7 metres (23 feet), how far below the surface of the water will the anchor be?

138. What has teeth but can't eat or speak? It can tear things apart and then bring them back together.

139. Jimmy spun in a circle, then turned right and then turned left. He did a forward roll and finally walked three steps backwards before rather dizzily taking a photograph of the sunset. What direction was he pointing in?

140. What falls but never breaks, and what breaks but never falls?

141. When does 9 + 4 = 1?

142. What part of your body can you hold in your left hand but not your right?

143. I shave every day, but my beard keeps getting longer. Who am I?

144. I come in many shades and you can prune me but I'll keep on growing. Keep an eye on me - one day I might disappear entirely! What am I?

145. What sometimes runs, but never walks, and sticks by you through and through?

146. You can see me clearly if you look in the right place, but I'm not really there. Everything I do is the opposite of you. What am I?

148. In 1066 there was the Norman Conquest. In 1776 the Declaration of Independence was signed. What happened in 1961 and will not happen again until 6009?

149. Can you make the letters
in 'new door' into one word?

150. What one thing do only happy people need, and if you eat it, you'll die?

151. What is made of water, but will die if you put it in a bath?

Answers

1. A rope

2. A phone

3. Their aunt is Matilda's mum

4. A pair of shoes

5. Alfie has the longest pencil

6. She's still near the bottom of the ladder

7. The two sons are from a set of triplets (or more!)

8. Short

9. You can't hide anything between pages 79 and 80 of a book – they are different sides of the same piece of paper.

10. Shake hands

11. A clock

12. Your breath

13. Yes, with a matchstick.

14. A pair of glasses

15. Nine: 4 + 5 = 9

16. A coat of paint

17. Polar bears live near the North Pole. This one has walked in a straight line: first it walked 5 kilometres (3.1 miles) north towards the North Pole, and then it continued for 4 more kilometres (2.5 miles) in the same direction, except now it's heading south. In total it travelled 9 kilometres (5.6 miles).

18. The ocean

19. It's not to one side of her, so it's on her other side!

20. A coin

21. A zebra

22. She needed a haircut!

23. The tide

24. Envelope

25. Fire

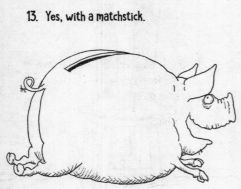

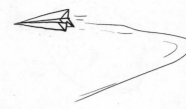

6. Potatoes. Pot + 8 Os

7. A sweater

8. A snail

9. They're facing inwards, looking across the tower towards each other.

0. It wasn't raining.

1. Seventy

2. A decimal point. If you put one between 5 and 6 you'd get 5.6, which is bigger than 5 but smaller than 6.

3. Hair

4. Any number. If you double a number and then multiply it by four you are multiplying it by eight. Dividing it by eight will get you the original number again.

5. A towel

6. One – after that the box isn't empty anymore.

7. Any animal – buildings can't jump!

8. A keyboard

9. None – it's a blackberry bush.

40. A hiccup

41. Silence

42. A shoe

43. Kerepakupai Merú – it was always the tallest waterfall in the world, even before it was discovered.

44. A lighthouse

45. Top secret

46. Nellie is 12. In two years' time she will be 14, and five years ago she was seven. Two times seven is 14.

47. In the dictionary

48. 9 kilometres (5.6 miles). It doesn't matter how fast everyone else is going!

49. Friday

50. Your father

51. A river

52. Neither – they will both be the same distance from Edinburgh when they pass each other.

53. The seven seas

54. Three and a half minutes – you just fry four at once!

55. Noise

56. Neither sentence is correct – halves are equal, there is no bigger or biggest half.

57. An alarm clock

58. A castle. The halo of water is the moat, the tongue of wood is the drawbridge and the skin of stone is the castle walls.

59. Forty

60. The smallest number of toadstools is three: red, white, white.

61. Water

62. There are 12 'seconds' in a year – January 2nd, February 2nd and so on.

63. Seven. She sold four apples to the first customer (half of seven is three and a half, plus a half = four apples), two to the second customer (there are three apples remaining and half of three is one and a half. Add the other half = two apples). The third customer had one apple.
Four + two + one = seven.

64. Thunderbolt (Th under bolt)

65. Rain

66. A glove

67. Pull out the plug.

68. A joke

69. Her sister is ten. Half of eight is four, so Florence's sister is four years younger than her. So when Florence is 14, her sister will be ten.

70. Grape

71. They're computer mice, not real mice.

72. The carpet

73. The third door – if it hasn't eaten for four years the tiger will be dead.

74. Tomorrow

75. Glass

76. Every hour the snail moves forward one brick in total, so it takes 12 hours to reach the top of the wall.

77. Seven – remove the 's' and it becomes 'even.'

78. Dan

1. Clockwise – it doesn't really matter which hand you are using, but you do need to hold the screw still.

2. Time

3. It would take 51 days.

4. A human being. It crawls when it is a baby, then walks on two legs, and needs a stick when it is older.

5. A lioness: take away the 'l', 'i' and both 's's and the word 'one' is left. The lion is the king of the jungle, so the lioness is the queen.

6. A chair

7. An hour and a half – you give one, wait half an hour, then give another and wait half an hour, then another, and wait another half an hour – and then the final pill. That's an hour and a half in total.

8. Fallen leaves

9. A hole

88. Yesterday, today and tomorrow

89. A bottle

90. She's wearing a uniform.

91. Paper

92. The letter V

93. 20 times

94. Money

95. Fun – the other words sound like letters ('U' and 'R').

96. A cold

97. A tooth

98. A mirror

99. Melon and lemon

100. Darkness

101. A jigsaw piece

102. A kiwi

103. 127 carrots – the number of carrots doubles every day, so one on Monday, two on Tuesday, four on Wednesday, eight on Thursday, 16 on Friday, 32 on Saturday and 64 on Sunday. If you add them all together you reach 127.

104. Homework

105. A compass

106. A cauliflower

107. Race car

108. A deck of cards

109. A road

110. Everything on the menu has to have double letters next to each other.

111. The wind

112. 20

113. Trouble

114. Heroine

115. A teapot

116. A swallow

117. Your age

118. You are!

119. An arrow

120. A screwdriver

121. When you say, 'I is the letter before in the alphabet.'

122. A sieve

123. Cat: It's one third of cow – 'c' – and half goat – 'at'

124. Stars

125. Today is the 1st January, and Mo's birthday is the 31st December. Mo wa 12 the day before yesterday (the 30 December), then turned 13 the next day. This year on the 31st December he'll turn 14, so next year he'll turn 1

126. The letter e

127. An onion

128. First Jack rowed the chicken across and came back. Then he rowe the dragon across. This time, when he came back, he brought the chicken with him. Then he rowed the grain across, leaving the chicken on the riverbank. He left the grain with the dragon, and came back, collecting the chicken and rowing across again. Then they all reached the other side safely.

THE WORLD'S BEST BOOK OF RIDDLES

?9. Snow

50. There are four feet in the barn – Albert has two and Kate has two. The other animals have paws or hooves.

51. Potato – chop off 'ato' and you're left with the word 'pot'.

52. Friendship

53. The moon

54. A mushroom

55. A broom

56. Phil, Sally, Sophie, Matthew.

57. 1 metre (3.2 feet) – it doesn't matter what the tide level is.

58. A zip

59. West, because the Sun sets in the West.

50. Night falls but never breaks and day breaks but never falls.

141. On a clock

142. Your right elbow

143. A barber

144. Hair

145. Your nose

146. Your reflection

147. Sawdust

148. In 1961, the year looks the same the right way up as it does upside down – and the same goes for 6009.

149. Simple, just rearrange them: one word.

150. Nothing

151. An ice cube

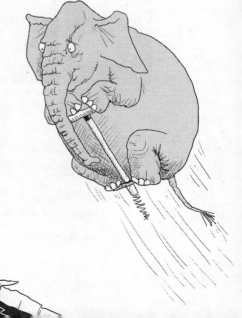

ALSO AVAILABLE:

ISBN: 978-1-78055-907-0

ISBN: 978-1-78055-908-7

ISBN: 978-1-78055-784-7

ISBN: 978-1-78055-785-4

ISBN: 978-1-78055-943-8

ISBN: 978-1-78055-963-6

ISBN: 978-1-78055-626-0

ISBN: 978-1-78055-624-6

ISBN: 978-1-78055-625-3

ISBN: 978-1-78055-964-3

ISBN: 978-1-78055-965-0

ISBN: 978-1-78055-635-2

ISBN: 978-1-78055-816-5